How Can I Keep From Singing

S·I·N·G·I·N·G?

THOUGHTS ABOUT LITURGY FOR MUSICIANS

How Can I Keep From
S·I·N·G·I·N·G?
THOUGHTS ABOUT LITURGY FOR MUSICIANS

Gabe Huck

Liturgy Training Publications

Design by Jill Smith.

Printed in the United States of America.
ISBN 0-930467-90-6

Contents

Much of what has made its way to these pages took shape first for three presentations at the 1986 Liturgical Music Workshop at Saint John's University, Collegeville, Minnesota. Parts of the first two chapters later appeared in *Liturgy 80* magazine. I am grateful to the staff of the Workshop for their gracious invitation to a nonmusician. The wonderful illustrations on the cover and pages of this book are the work of Mozelle Thompson. They were originally published in a book for children, *Lift Every Voice and Sing,* the story and text of the song by James Weldon Johnson that is often called the national anthem of African-Americans.

—Gabe Huck

Chapter 1

What Kind of a Thing Is the Liturgy?

n the summer of 1985, I was one of two dozen participants in a three-day conversation about liturgy and music. On the final evening, our group joined with a cathedral full of people to listen to choirs from various parishes. The whole assembly joined in singing some of the pieces while other compositions were performed by single choirs or combinations of choirs. It was a marvelous gathering.

When our group came together the next morning for a last session, the music and experience of the night before were in everyone's thoughts, and this led to an

interesting exchange. Some spoke of the experience of
the previous evening as an inspiring sample of what
good liturgy is meant to be. Others were equally taken
with the spirit and beauty of what had happened, but
they wanted to call the event a festival or a concert,
not a liturgy. It was uplifting, it was praise to God, it
was prayer. It was not liturgy.

The confusion here extends to most of us and it is
about far more than definitions. It is about what sort of
a deed liturgy is. This particular event did much of
what we generally ask of liturgy. Hearts were lifted.
Voices were united. There was a sense of community
that was strong and delightful, and this was not just
any community but one founded on a shared faith and
shared expression of that faith. We should all be so
lucky as to have Sunday mornings where such things
happen.

What difference then what we call it? A rose by any
other name, right? But no matter how many people call
a rose an oak tree, the rose does not become an oak.
An oak is one thing, a rose another. Having different

names not only helps to keep them straight, it says that we understand the difference and we can think about and act toward each in an appropriate manner.

The challenge is not to find the right name for that delightful experience of people and music. The challenge is with us and with how we think about the liturgy. What is it we imagine when we imagine the liturgy of the church? We often speak and act as if a good liturgy were a cluster of just those fine things named above: uplifted hearts, bonds of community, strengthened faith. Try completing this sentence in no more than 25 words: "A good liturgy on a Sunday morning in my parish would be one in which . . ." (What variety we might find around us if we let the way people are actually doing Sunday liturgy be their statement!)

What do we observe in the week-by-week practice of our parishes? We see liturgy understood as devotion, as occasion for the prayer of individuals that is sincere

What Kind of a Thing Is the Liturgy?

and deep. We see liturgy as education, as opportunity for clergy and others to speak volumes, well or badly, to a rare captive audience. We see liturgy as therapy, the ministers' weekly opportunity to care for the bedraggled people from the trenches of the homes and offices and factories of weekday life. We see liturgy as affirmation, mostly affirmation of our wonderful, ever-wounded, ever-healed selves. We see liturgy as the mechanical performance of directions. And we see— and the contrast is what makes it so refreshing— liturgy as something like that festival, liturgy done to uplift, inspire, strengthen and bring forth prayer.

Each of these approaches to liturgy has its appropriate sounds and words of music. But do any of them give a satisfactory conclusion to our sentence? "A good liturgy on a Sunday morning in my parish would be one in which . . ."

Environment and Art in Catholic Worship, a 1978 document of the Bishops' Committee on the Liturgy of the United States Catholic Conference, offers this two-sentence description of the liturgy:

6

Each church gathers regularly to praise and thank God, to remember and make present God's great deeds, to offer common prayer, to realize and celebrate the kingdom of peace and justice. That action of the Christian assembly is liturgy.

Most of our "good liturgy in 25 words or less" would have touched on some of those verbs: gather, praise, thank, remember, offer, celebrate. What might have been missing in our descriptions, and what separated the two sides of that discussion, is not so much the verbs but the noun and the adverb: "Each church gathers regularly to . . ." The noun, the subject, is "the church." The adverb, the way all those verbs are done, is "regularly."

Often our notions of liturgy have us doing something *for* or *to* the people. But liturgy can only be what that people, that church, that local assembly, does *as an assembly*. Even more, liturgy can only be what that church does *regularly*. Liturgy, then, can only be what that church knows how to do, has it in its heart and mind and muscles to do. Liturgy can only be what that

What Kind of a Thing Is the Liturgy?

church knows by heart. Liturgy is something the church does, something that each child and each catechumen grows into, receives, treasures.

There is a problem, then, when we act as if the liturgy is good when people leave impressed, inspired, healed or educated. None of those things are really of first importance. What does matter is that people leave having done the thing they have been doing since childhood, doing it yet again, doing it carefully and reverently, doing it with awe and yet competence, doing it not only because they want to (because they might not particularly want to on any given Sunday), but finally and essentially because they need to.

Certain aspects of our culture suggest that we are going to find it particularly difficult to move toward a liturgy that is the deed of all the assembled, baptized people. In *Amusing Ourselves to Death,* Neil Postman argues that the pervasive presence of television has changed most of what was public and communal life into entertainment. Politics, sports, even the weather become commodities to entertain us. "There's no business *but* show business," he concludes. Do we wonder why people on Sunday can so easily expect to be an audience and why presiders and musicians come to think of their tasks as quite close to entertaining (to think of themselves as, in fact, in competition with the television for people's interest)? Do we wonder why we want something new each Sunday or why we worry about getting their attention and hoping that they leave with just a little insight and a little uplift and just a bit of community?

Musicians and other artists are in special danger here for it is easy for them to put their skills at the service of this entertainment mode and to feel that the work has been done well when compliments are received. The words of the compliments may tell more than we should want to hear. This "here-I-am-entertain-me" way of life will not be dealt with simply by convincing people that liturgy is different. Something like conversion is at stake. The kind of singing, listening, pondering, blessing, interceding, communing that our liturgy demands will not coexist with lives that do not sing, listen, ponder, bless, intercede and commune day by day and year by year.

If it is the church that does the liturgy, this local church in communion with its bishop, then that is why the adverb must be "regularly." Liturgy cannot be a one-time event or a now-and-again occurrence. To be liturgy it has to be done over and over and over again. If the presider "does" the liturgy, or the musicians or the homilist or anyone else, then we are talking about something where each Sunday will be judged on its own merits, like a concert or a lecture. (What all of these ministers do matters, matters greatly—just as what the cook does and what the waiter does matters at a meal. But the meal is not a meal because there happened to be a good cook or an excellent waiter. We make it a meal, we who sit down together.)

The very simple thing behind all of this is that we have to treat liturgy like the kind of thing it is, and that is the sort of human activity we call ritual.

Ritual gets all manner of bad press. There is just a hint of something meaningless, something thoughtless, something demeaning. Why do we think this way? Perhaps, first of all, because ritual, like all the basic stuff of human life, can be twisted and abused. That happens with eating, it happens with sleeping. And it happens with ritual in the hands of the totalitarian state, the despotic teacher or parent, even one's own psyche. Ritual patterns can become tools of oppression. At other times, we have known ritual as a substitute for engagement: rote learning instead of grappling and ownership of knowledge. Thus, for many, ritual implies an absence of human involvement, an absence of meaning. They have a baby-with-the-bath-water reaction that affects a sense for liturgy.

We can admit that ritual is risky and that it can be abused, then move on to a new understanding and appreciation of the potential for good in ritual deeds.

Because liturgy is ritual, we have that word "regularly" in any worthy description of liturgy. Only when we are comfortable with this can we grasp that whole description of liturgy quoted above and see this clearly: For the liturgy to be deeds done by the church—all that gathering, listening, praising, acknowledging—the deeds have to be done with great regularity.

Musicians should know about this in at least two ways. First, music itself is built on the good use of repetition, the need for rhythm, for pattern. Second, the love of music implies that one accepts what wonders there are in something that does not wear out with repetition but opens the one who knows it to beauty and understanding. What is that bond that can exist between musician and music, doer and deed, when the composition is known—and these two words are good and important—*by heart*?

Musicians know also about our culture's fear of

repetition, our throw-away society's drive to devour the new. We are better trained in consuming than in savoring. How else will there be a market for next year's songs, records and hymnals?

The sort of knowing by heart that is involved in doing liturgy means that the things that we do— hearing, speaking, singing, moving—must be such that they can bear the repetition. That is a terrible demand. Rather than face it, we go scurrying for something new. With the new we can entertain, inspire, educate, even heal. What we fail to do is to find and give the sustaining nourishment that we can take week by week and season by season until it is truly ours, our own, by heart.

Our rituals—and they must extend far beyond the liturgy itself to embrace many customs of individuals, households and communities—are the shaping and measure of our lives. If we know by heart how to gather, how to hear the word and intercede for all the world, how to give thanks and praise to God over the bread and wine, how to take communion, how to separate from one another, we would little by little be shaped by these deeds. Little by little, these acts would be images of our whole lives.

All of this is not to say that we should not want a liturgy that engenders a strong sense of community or inspires positive feelings and concerns for justice. But liturgy must do this as liturgy and, therefore, as ritual. That is the only kind of human activity that liturgy can honestly be. To treat liturgy as something that is at our whim, something to be filled with well-meaning efforts to do good things (for inspiring, educating and stimulating toward just deeds are all good), is to lose the liturgy. What is done instead may be good for today, but never, never capable of carrying the church, shaping Christians, belonging to the people.

If liturgy is ritual, if it is the ritual deed of the people, then it is not our plaything. We have received it and it is ours to do according to its own demands and then to hand on. It is not an hour or so on Sunday to fill as we see fit. Rather, it is to be the "by heart" deed of the community, the church: Gathering is, listening is, interceding is, blessing is, communion is, scattering is.

So it comes down to these two things. One: Rituals (and all of liturgy is ritual) are done by the people. Two: The people who do their rituals do them by heart.

Are there leaders? Yes, but anyone who leads at liturgy ministers. The leader is one of the assembly and remains part of the assembly, but serves the assembly with the singing of psalm verses, the reading of a text, the hospitality tasks, the preaching or the presiding. Does "by heart" mean that everyone would ideally know every word, every movement? No, but it means that the assembly knows the texture and the movement of its liturgy. The assembly knows how to listen to the reading of scripture, how to savor the refrain of a psalm, how to acclaim the gospel. And the assembly knows the order and the flow of these things. There is no audience. At plays and at rallies, the people are important, but they are reacting with and supporting actors and speakers. Here at liturgy it is different. The people are the actors and the ministers serve them in various roles. The interaction is in all directions and it includes looking and touching and moving.

Aidan Kavanagh makes this point with strength and humor. He is speaking of pews, but the point applies to much else that we do *for* and *to* people when we organize the liturgy without recognizing what liturgy itself is.

> Pews, which entered liturgical place only recently, nail the assembly down, proclaiming that the liturgy is not a common action but a preachment perpetrated upon the seated, an ecclesiastical opera done by virtuosi for a paying audience. Pews distance the congregation, disenfranchise the faithful, and rend the assembly. Filling a church with immovable pews is similar to placing bleachers directly on a basketball court: It not only interferes with movement but changes the event

into something entirely different. *Elements of Rite* (New York: Pueblo Publishing Company), 21.

Clearly pews have their equivalent in other dimensions of the liturgy. What else do we do that proclaims, as pews do, that what happens here is for an audience? What else that we do denies, as pews do, that this is a *common* action? What else that we do distances the congregation and disenfranchises (takes away the voice and vote) the faithful and rends the assembly (divides it into the doers and the watchers, or into the doers and the active watchers and the passive watchers)? What else that we do changes the nature of the event? Consider Kavanagh's bleachers on a basketball court. If we didn't know what was supposed to happen at a basketball game, we might very well put the bleachers on the court. If we don't know what is supposed to happen at a liturgy, we might do a lot of what we are doing now. The problem is not always a lack of money or skill or good intentions or hard work. The problem may just be not knowing how to *think about* the liturgy.

Chapter 2

At Home with Ritual

t helps to discover what we know already about ritual, what we have experienced and observed outside the liturgy of the church. Often we can bring these insights back and see the liturgy and our own tasks in a new way.

Here is a brief story from a different place, time and culture. Ask of it: What is ritual? What makes it happen? Why can it bear repetition? Why do its celebrants seek repetition? The text is from the auto-biography of Bella Chagall. She is telling her memories of childhood in a Jewish home in turn-of-the-century Russia. Listen to her, an adult remembering Friday nights at home when the Sabbath (Shabbes) was to arrive any moment. Dwell for a while in this story of one part of one ritual. Make a list of all that you find going into the ritual.

The last to leave the shop is mother. She tries all the doors once more to see that they are locked. Now I hear her pattering steps. Now she shuts the metal door of the rear shop. Now her dress rustles. Now her soft shoes slip into the dining room. In the doorway she halts for a moment: the white table with the silver candlesticks dazzles her eyes. At once she begins to hurry. She quickly washes her face and hands, puts on a clean lace collar that she always wears on this night, and approaches the candlesticks like a quite new mother. With a match in her hand she lights one candle after another. All the seven candles begin to quiver. The flames blaze into mother's face. As though an enchantment were falling upon her, she lowers her eyes. Slowly, three times in succession, she encircles the candles with both her arms; she seems to be taking them into her heart. And with the candles her weekday worries melt away. She blesses the candles. She whispers quiet benedictions through her fingers and they add heat to the flames. Mother's hands over the candles shine like the tablets of the decalogue over the holy ark.

I push closer to her. I want to get behind her blessing hands myself. I seek her face. I want to look into her eyes. They are concealed behind her spread-out fingers.

I light my little candle by mother's candle. Like her, I raise my hands and through them, as through a gate, I murmur into my little candle flame the words of benediction that I catch from my mother.

My candle, just lighted, is already dripping. My hands circle it to stop its tears.

I hear mother in her benedictions mention now one name, now another. She names father, the children, her own father and mother. Now my name too has fallen into the flame of the candles. My throat becomes hot.

"May the Highest One give them his blessing!" concludes
mother, dropping her hands at last.

"Amen," I say in a choking voice, behind my fingers.

"Good shabbes!" mother calls out loudly. Her face, all
opened, looks purified. I think that it has absorbed the
illumination of the Sabbath candles.   *Burning Lights*
(New York: Schocken Books, 1962), 48–49.

The author goes on to tell of other aspects of the
meal, of the evening that follows and of the way
the Sabbath was kept in their home. But even the few
paragraphs quoted suggest some important elements of
ritual:

▶ There is a place, a room. It is not a space where
only this happens, but it is clearly the space where
this *always* happens. If Sabbath is to be welcomed,
here is where we welcome it. What makes it so? Years
of doing it. The room is home to these deeds. (And yet
there is a sense that should misfortune of any sort

deprive the family of this place, the Sabbath would be fittingly welcomed wherever they might be.)

▶ There are things: the table and its cloth, the foods, the candlesticks and candles of melting wax, a special garment.

▶ There are movements, gestures, postures: entering, washing, dressing, lighting candles, encircling, covering the eyes. With this goes the seeing: of others, of all this being done, of the objects.

▶ There are words: the blessing words, blessing of God, intercession for friends and family. These are not new words each week, but old and new as needed, mostly learned from a parent and slowly evolving.

▶ There is time itself. This is at the very center of things for it is the coming of darkness on the sixth day of the week that draws the little assembly and causes the remembering, the keeping of the commandment to do this, to hallow this time, to lay aside all that is of the week and to welcome into home and life the very presence of God in time.

In all of these we find those two elements of ritual we have been exploring:

▶ Rituals are the deeds of people. Some may have one thing to do, some another, but no one is audience. The whole ritual belongs to everyone.

▶ Rituals are done by heart. Everyone knows the flow, has the movements in their bones, the tunes in their vocal chords, the words on their lips, the smells in their nostrils, the sights in their eyes. Texts may change with seasons or special days, but the order everyone knows as they know how to breathe.

What is the good work that ritual can do, work so good that we seek it despite the dangers? Ritual's work is this: Through the measures of time— day by day, week by week, season by season, year by year, and also those measures of time that come from passage through life—a people may find their own self, their own soul. The ritual is a poor human thing made up of what arts we have: sound, movements, things, sharing food and sharing fasting, telling stories, singing words, and the good ordering of all these things. The rite itself can be as simple as the sign of the cross or as complex as that whole assembling of practices that constitute passage from outside to inside the church in the church's restored rites of Christian initiation.

These rituals of ours come in every rhythm that life and the body and the tribe have: the rhythm of the day and night, the rhythm of eating and hunger, the rhythm of work and rest (daily and in the invented cycle of our week), the rhythm of birth and growth and death, the rhythm of the seasons, the rhythm of conversion and initiation. The church has its rituals to mark rising and retiring, the gathering at table, days of fasting and charity, Sundays and festivals, death and birth and weddings, the initiation of new members and the reconciliation of old members.

If these are ours, ours through their repetition, ours through their good use of human arts, then we can say that (to borrow a phrase from those who have studied the anthropology and sociology of human ritual) our rituals are a kind of rehearsal.

Think about the sign of the cross as such a rehearsal. Over and over it comes—from the door of the church before baptism, through each morning and night at bedside, each Sunday in the assembly, then to the anointing of the body in sickness and in the end the signing of the body for burial with that same cross. What are we rehearsing? In that cross traced over and over, we are learning the very shape of our lives, knowing or absorbing little by little how for us that cross is the weapon against evil and the victory over death. This is not a matter of theology, first, but of muscles, the body, the whole person.

Another example is the fast before communion. Though now very brief, it is still a ritual and so a rehearsal. It is practicing how all life is anticipation, is all the "not yet" of the kingdom of God, is all a waiting, a looking forward, a hunger.

Our rituals are the necessarily slow ways of becoming ourselves, becoming this people. They are like a home for us, a place where we find out how to be us. In a pastoral letter on the liturgy, Cardinal Joseph Bernardin wrote of the ritual of holy communion:

> At this table we put aside every worldly separation based on culture, class, or other differences. Baptized, we no longer admit to distinctions based on age or sex or race or wealth. This communion is why all prejudice, all racism, all sexism, all deference to wealth and power must be banished from our parishes, our homes, and our lives. This communion is why we will not call enemies those who are human beings like ourselves. This communion is why we will not commit the world's resources to an escalating arms race while the poor die. We cannot. Not when we have feasted here on the "body broken" and the "blood poured out" for the life of the world. Let that be clear in the reverent way we walk forward to take the holy bread

and cup. Let it be clear in the way ministers of
communion announce: "The body of Christ," "The
blood of Christ." Let it be clear in our "Amen." Let it
be clear in the songs and psalms we sing and the way
we sing them. Let it be clear in the holy silence that
fills this church when all have partaken.

That is the way it is with ritual. What we do over and
over, do by heart, is the rehearsal of life, the embodi-
ment in sound and gesture and all our arts of who we
mean to be.

As such, there is always an edge to ritual properly
practiced by us, an edge because it is only rehearsal
and because of what it is rehearsing. We feel that edge
when we sit down to full tables and must give thanks
to God. We feel that edge—as the quote from Cardinal
Bernardin indicates—when we come to a table where
every worldly separation is put aside, yet we do not
put them aside. We feel that edge when we ask the
ritual questions of catechumens: "Do you
renounce . . . ?" Is this a game, an empty form,
something from antiquity without any meaning? Or is

it a very painful chafing of ourselves against what we are not yet, can in fact hardly face? In a remarkably similar way, that edge to ritual is there in the person who stops whatever is being done because a bell is ringing and begins to recite: "The angel of the Lord . . ." However docile such a one may seem to the world's powers, there is—in the way this prayer comes around day by day, year-in and year-out—a limit placed on any power in this world.

Ritual that is this sort of rehearsal clashes with some of the ways planners and ministers have treated the liturgy. We have often acted as if the liturgy had to pay great attention to us, to our moods and feelings. But if our ritual is this rehearsal, it has more to do with training me about how to be than mirroring how I feel. Rituals are a lot like that kiss which wives and husbands may exchange each morning before separating for the day. It is a kiss, but it is a ritual too. The moment is not for casting around for some word, some gesture, some song, something that will speak of how I am feeling today about our relationship, about myself, about life in general. It is just done, this kiss. It is the gesture of what I *mean*, not of what I feel. It is the rehearsal of what I mean and believe as husband or wife. So is the sign of the cross a rehearsal of what I mean and believe as a baptized Catholic. So is the whole of Christian initiation. So is Sunday liturgy. Yet too often we let the greetings, music, homilies cater to momentary feelings of leaders and assemblies rather than serve that essential task of training our lips and hearts, each one of us and all together.

Liturgy then is ritual activity. It is that sort of human activity where we use the tools of human expression—words, sounds, gestures, objects, order— use them over and over again in various rhythms to embody and express and learn what we mean and believe.

It is important to recognize that our repertory of ritual extends far beyond the liturgy: the keeping of seasons, for example, or morning and night and meal prayers, or Friday fasting and charity as called for in the bishops' pastoral letter on peace. Yet here is a serious problem for all involved with the public liturgy of the church. As Catholic Christians living in North America in the last years of the 20th century, we have precious few rituals. As Americans, we have lots. As consumers, we have lots. As mostly middle-class people, we have lots. These too are rehearsals, training us to mean and believe in ways that are often in conflict with the course set at baptism. But as Catholic Christians, the Sunday gathering and a few other rites come to bear the entire weight, and they cannot—even in the best of times.

The acclamation sung at the supper table is what would accustom us to the acclamation sung at the Sunday eucharistic table. The table itself as the physical and regular gathering point for exchange and nourishment would accustom us to the Sunday table. The day by day signing with the cross and recital of God's praise would accustom us to what we are to do together on Sunday. When all of this becomes a matter of taste, then it is no wonder that those who still assemble on Sunday often have none of the words, the tunes, the art they need to do this liturgy, to make it theirs.

Perhaps we turn to the liturgy as inspiration or as therapy precisely because we do not know how to handle this devastating cultural situation. Certainly the shape given to life by the gospel has always clashed with the times, but our own day seems particularly difficult. Some insight into this comes from the studies of sociologist Robert Bellah. In *Habits of the Heart,* he looks primarily at that strata of American society where most Catholics are to be found. Bellah and his associates describe a triumph of individualism, individualism cut loose from the balancing demands of community that in earlier generations had produced the characteristic genius of our culture. For most of us, the family has come to be the only community, and the family cannot bear such a burden. It too breaks down. The freedom in whose name such individualism is championed becomes strangely without content. It is total—and totally empty. In the end, those who have the advantages to construct such autonomous lives do not end up strong individuals at all, but consumers of the latest styles in politics, food and goods. In such a time, it is understandable that we grab for the liturgy as a tool, a way to affirm community and self, a way to raise consciousness or convey a positive self-image. We come to liturgy as products of the culture.

So there is going to be a collision. When we want the liturgy to be ritual for us, what will happen? We are going to crash right into this culture. Our ritual is an expression of an ordered freedom, of individuals living within the discipline of a tradition, the discipline of a community. Perhaps it comes down to a story about a Catholic funeral in New England a few years ago where they sang, at the communion, "I did it

my way." If the gentleman who was being buried did it
his way, we had no business burying him our way.
That is what it means to call the liturgy our ritual and
to abide by that.

Chapter 3

"Musical Liturgy" Is Redundant

There are certainly rituals without music: a sign of the cross made on the forehead of a child as a night blessing, the keeping of Friday with fasting and charity. But when many people come together for ritual, we expect there to be music. Huub Oosterhuis has written:

What goes much farther than the spoken word is everything that is sung. The speaking voice interprets and narrows down human experience, the song (for one voice, for several voices, sung in verses or antiphonally, short as a cry or long-winded as a hymn) is broader and goes deeper. . . .

A song is more guileless, joyful, effective and human than any way of speaking. A song may be admonitory, instructive and catechetic, but *if it is good, it is always more than this.* The sung word is the very heart of the liturgy.

Singing is discovered and invented, it is born at times when there is no other possible way for people to express themselves—at the grave, for example, when four or five people with untrained, clumsy voices sing words that are greater and smaller than their faith and their experience. *Prayers, Poems and Songs* (New York: Herder and Herder, 1970), 103–4. [Emphasis added.]

The song frequently led by Pete Seeger asks the same question: "How can I keep from singing?" Now that might seem no question at all to the frustrated parish music director, but it does get to the heart of the matter. Song is broader and goes deeper than any other use of words. It is what we *need:* not a luxury, not a frill, not an obligation, but a need. If there is to be ritual, if there is to be anything at the graveside or around the wedding couple or at tableside on Sunday, the human voice must go higher and lower, faster and slower than our speaking can be. It must have the patterns and the rhythms, must know itself as taken up into the sound many together make, must find this human art that is itself the discipline of community.

The German pastor, theologian and martyr Dietrich Bonhoeffer posed the question for himself: Why do Christians sing when they are together? He replied:

> The reason is, quite simply, because in singing together it is possible for them to speak and pray the same word at the same time; in other words, because here they can unite in the Word. . . . It is the voice of the church that is heard in singing together. It is not you that sings, it is the church that is singing, and you, as a member of the church, may share in its song. Thus all singing together that is right must serve to widen our spiritual horizon, make us see our little company as a member

of the great Christian church on earth, and help us
willingly and gladly to join our singing, be it feeble or
good, to the song of the church.   *Life Together* (New
York: Harper and Row, 1954), 59.

"How can I keep from singing?" Bonhoeffer answers: If
baptized, you can't. If you have cast your lot with this
church, if you have been hounded inside, you can't.
Our ritual song is a rehearsal for life. I do not come to
explore my own wounds or joys or anxieties, but rather
to learn my part. I do so with the melodies that
become my own vocabulary. Are they then foreign to
those wounds, joys and anxieties? Rather, they are
more.

We sing because this is the nature of the ritual we
do together. If all kept silence throughout, that would
be a ritual, Quaker-like, but not the tradition we know.
Our tradition has deeds that need music (processions,
for example) and words that need music (acclamations
and refrains that have nothing to do with the speaking
voices of an assembly).

s this how we approach the music of our liturgy? So often it is rather as something added on, something to go behind the actions of the ministers, something to fill up moments between speaking, something to engage the people or move them. All in all, we act too often as if we knew very well how to keep from singing. Singing seems to be the challenge, not holding back.

But if liturgy is what we baptized do, week by week, what we do because we need to, and if liturgy so done is what forms us into what the baptismal plunge proclaimed, then the liturgy is sung because that's all we have. There is a place for silence and a place for plain speaking, but singing is all we have when it comes time to acclaim, to intercede, to process. Oosterhuis would say that singing is the only way to make a sound at such a moment. Bonhoeffer would say that singing is the only way to act together, to be the church and not so many individuals. What should be sung but is left unsung will not be simply stifled, kept inside, frustrated. What is unsung will not be.

Some years ago the saying was popular among liturgists and musicians: "Musical liturgy is normative." It made a point: The common, the normal, the usual and expected form of liturgy involved song. Anything else is *not* normal. What could have been said of our tradition is: Musical liturgy is a redundancy. Saying "musical liturgy" is like saying "multicolored rainbow." It is liturgy's nature to be sung. Our song is something without which there would be no liturgy.

When we come expecting to do and not to watch, we will need our music, our song. Song becomes an extra, only nice or only pretty, when we come for inspiration, entertainment, obligation or education. But if we come to do, then song is central to the whole undertaking, for the task to be done can't be done except in song.

That's not in the cultural grain. We go against that

grain when we assemble not at our convenience but at the time set for the whole community. We go against that grain again when we expect nothing from the liturgy yet put everything into it, and again when we try to make of liturgy a deed where there is no star and no audience, no spectator and no spectacle. Is it any wonder that this does not come easily? We found it easier to let music be cute or catchy or impressive. That was enough to bring gratitude from the departing congregation. We all sense how truly radical (going for the roots) it will be to buckle down for the long haul and say: Face it, this isn't about making people feel good or holy or even kind. This is basic training in living like a baptized person, life and death stuff, and so cut the frills and get down to the business of singing our liturgy.

Chapter 4

Surrounded by Music, Robbed of Song

To ask about music's work in this ritual of ours is to ask about music and ourselves. Certainly, we have music as people have never before had music. Walk the streets of a city and count on seeing people with stereos in their ears on their way to work, out jogging, walking the dog. Make a call, get put on hold and hear "easy listening" music. Elevator music is a cliché. The supermarket plays music to shop by, wonderful Beatles' tunes ruined by a hundred sentimental strings. MTV tries to make music visual. Records and tapes and compact disks fill stores.

The symphonies have their marathons and summer becomes the sound of street musicians and festivals. Commercials command the services of some of the more creative writers of tunes and lyrics and we all end up humming little tributes about "This Bud's for you" or "Be all that you can be." These are our American acclamations and refrains.

Other than these jingles, an occasional "Star-Spangled Banner" and here and there a "Happy Birthday," we don't actually sing much of anything ourselves. Most of us know music as listeners and observers. A few know music as performers, entertainers of others. For all the music around us, singing together is no longer part of normal public life, except perhaps the crowd at the ballpark with their very limited repertory.

Are there still lullabies that parents sing to their children? Are there catchy nursery rhymes and things like the alphabet song (but can you really sing along with "Sesame Street"?) and "Eency weency spider"? (If you think repetition isn't powerful, stop right here and sing that spider song—with the gestures!) Are there school songs? Parodies of school songs? Jump rope songs? Camp songs? Are there work songs? Prison songs? Are there Christmas carols that get sung live in homes? Are there protest songs sung by the people who protest?

It is not only this one ritual of ours—Sunday eucharist—that has its music, that must be sung. All sorts of regular moments, recurring moments, have had their songs, their tunes, their sounds. Do they still? Do they have these not as nostalgia and not as entertainment but as their own, as the very way we rock a baby, walk a picket line, begin a morning, end a year, keep a festival?

Consumers and watchers by conditioning, we are not doing so well. We retain, perhaps, some sense that it would take music to do the human thing when we sit bereaved by the death of a close friend or family member. But we don't have it in us anymore. We may sense that the reuniting of the family at Christmas would need song, even carols sung together, but what's known beyond the first verse? And when would we do it? Our addiction to the never-stopping stream of entertainment makes idle moments few.

Are we losing the habit of song in a world crammed full of music? Are we losing song that has an accustomed place, that is at home in a certain kind of moment, that makes this moment human and our own?

The matter of liturgy that is done, sung, by the assembly cannot be considered apart from who we are, we the assembly. Perhaps the text for this reflection should be from Psalm 137:

> By the streams of Babylon
>> we sat and wept
>> when we remembered Zion.
> On the aspens of that land
>> we hung up our harps,

Though there our captors asked of us
   the lyrics of our songs,
And our despoilers urged us to be joyous:
   "Sing for us the songs of Zion!"
How could we sing a song of the Lord
   in a foreign land?
If I forget you, Jerusalem,
   may my right hand be forgotten!
May my tongue cleave to my palate
   if I remember you not,
If I place not Jerusalem
   ahead of my joy.

How can we sing the Lord's song in a foreign land?
Our tradition would say that the land, the times, the
culture are *always* foreign to us. We are aliens all,
strangers and pilgrims, the "poor wayfaring stranger
traveling through this world of woe," the "poor
banished children of Eve mourning and weeping in
this valley of tears." And that is right. We are. Do we
know it? Do we recognize the particular foreignness of
our time and place?

How can we sing the Lord's song? For us, perhaps, this means: "How can we *sing* the Lord's song?" How can we sing—for we do not sing. How can we sing—for song is only to entertain and amuse. It seems no longer the stuff of human life, however tuneful or untuneful the person.

How can we *sing*? This means also: How can we sing when in some ways to look open-eyed at humankind today leads not to song but to silence? The times have changed. David Power speaks of us as living between the holocausts. What song is there in a land this foreign? Do we go on singing as if there had been no Auschwitz and no Hiroshima and as if there will be no nuclear winter? We must be very careful. There is song, but we can only learn it when we have faced what is evil in our times. Any effort to sing the Lord's song here will be tentative, only realistically done with some trembling.

The psalm says, "May my tongue cleave to my palate if I remember you not, if I place not Jerusalem ahead of my joy." May we be without any speech, any words, any song, except that we remember our God and Jerusalem, our home, the place that is not this place, the place we dimly remember. How shall we sing the Lord's song in a land that is foreign because it robs us of song and soothes us with entertaining music? That and not just the ideals of the documents and the images of earlier Christian worship must be our concern. To sing the liturgy of our church here, now, is to confront life and death. If we treat it as less, we have taken an unworthy path.

We are people in the midst of evil denouncing evil and affirming belief in this God who in various ways but especially in the cross and resurrection of Christ has sought us out. That is meant to be wrenching, hard, a constant hindrance to business as usual, to getting too comfortable here. We have to be poor enough to need music. When we get together to be the way we have believed in, when we assemble to remind ourselves of what God's reign is to be like (and, we say and believe, to remind God also), what music is there both to shatter our own cozy images of God's realm and to let us put our death and our life into tunes and words?

Partly, this is the music that the generations of our ancestors have given us, plainsong and polyphony, psalm tones and hymns, litanies and antiphons. Partly it is sounds not known to them, sounds born in our century.

How can we be a people who hunger so to sing this? Just think of what that would be like. In a time when you can play a tape of the *Exsultet*, play it whenever you wish, is it possible to long for that one moment a year when it is sung in the midst of the assembly? Or could you look forward to a single time each year the *Veni, Sancte Spiritus* is sung? Or to the short season of the Christmas sounds and words? What can a given assembly come to need? What is once a year, what is of a season, what is each week—if together this assembly is to have a vocabulary, a repertory, that it needs, truly needs, to voice its praise and thanks, intercession and sorrow, to voice these as constant attitudes, the very sound of being baptized persons, the sound that can sustain and shape a people, rehearse them to live in a foreign land?

One task of Christian ritual is to give us words and tunes that will be what we (our very baptized selves) sound like, dead as we are and yet putting on the Lord Jesus day by day, lifelong. That does not happen all at once, but over faithful years of doing our rituals, day by day and week by week and season by season. Here it must be that we find the words and tunes that have little to do with how we like them or how we are inspired by them. We must find the words and tunes we need, a matter of survival, life itself.

This means we must have song apart from the Sunday eucharist. Where is ritual and its song whenever members of a parish gather? There are the meetings of all kinds, the school, the religious education program, various groups for study and support and apostolic work, catechumenate, sacramental preparation meetings. And there is the domestic church, households at the dinner table, parents at bedsides with children.

This is not a matter of devising ever new ways to do prayer services or on-the-spot compositions. It is very much a matter of parish staff—beginning with their own meetings—having a sense for the prayer of the church as this has given meaning to morning, noon, evening, night. The rite should be brief, steady, usual, parochial, able to be known by heart after a few times. It should be rooted in how the church comes to the morning or the evening or the night and in how that is colored by the season or feast. It should use music (a hymn of a few stanzas, a single melodic line repeated over and over, a litany), simple forms good enough to bear the repetition and, even more, to thrive with the repetition.

Often we have been too elaborate in our designs, and then have given up when things do not work out. We need to be more simple, less ambitious. During the

Ordinary Time, night after night a family could include in its simple table blessing the same sung words, perhaps learning a variety of tunes. For example:

> Be present at our table, Lord,
> Be here and everywhere adored.
> Thy creatures bless and grant that we
> May feast in paradise with thee.

This is so simple and so strong, able to bear repetition. Such a piece gradually is ours. It is ours in exactly the way good ritual does its work. This means that neither word nor tune captures the moment exactly, captures just how anyone feels at the end of a given day. That does not matter. Word and tune are rather about what our lives mean, about who we are and are becoming.

Parish musicians have a work to do beyond the hours of liturgy and the place of assembly. They have resources needed for group and household ritual. Musicians have to do this for themselves, for the parish staff, slowly and steadily working out from there. (An excellent resource, one that makes limited use of song in attempting to be very realistic about what is possible, is *Catholic Household Blessings and Prayers*. This is an order of daily and occasional prayer for individuals and families. It is published by the United States Catholic Conference for the Bishops' Committee on the Liturgy and is available from Liturgy Training Publications.) If there is to be no Sunday assembly without music, music that is the assembly's as doer of the liturgy, and if this is a special challenge in our hard times, then we ought to see to it that gradually we are formed as a people who do sing, who possess tunes and words, acclamations and refrains, who know them by heart and gladly give voice to them in many settings.

Chapter 5

The Words

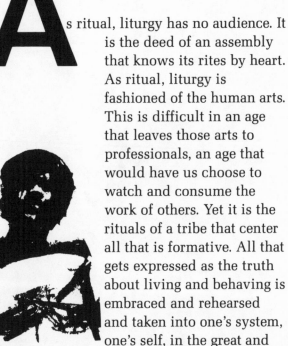

As ritual, liturgy has no audience. It is the deed of an assembly that knows its rites by heart. As ritual, liturgy is fashioned of the human arts. This is difficult in an age that leaves those arts to professionals, an age that would have us choose to watch and consume the work of others. Yet it is the rituals of a tribe that center all that is formative. All that gets expressed as the truth about living and behaving is embraced and rehearsed and taken into one's system, one's self, in the great and small rituals of the people.

It is almost an old soap opera question: What happens when, in a culture that seems to shape us as individual consumers, some persons seek to renew a liturgy that is about something quite different? Much of what we have experienced in the last 25 years has been a kind of capitulation of liturgy to the culture. Is it now possible to have some perspective?

Those who minister to a local assembly at their liturgy should ignore neither the nature of the liturgy nor the difficult situation we are in. We ignore liturgy's nature when we treat the liturgy as our private domain, when we treat the assembly as onlookers or consumers of inspiration or whatever we have to offer (even if what we have to offer is good stuff). We ignore the difficult cultural situation we are in when we empty the rites of their content because that gospel would be so little at home in this time and place.

We can consider all this by paying some attention to one of the arts by which liturgy lives, words.

How are words part of liturgy? How are words to be strong enough to do their work, to bear the weight of repetition, the weight of mystery and reverence? Begin with a poem by Anne Sexton:

> Be careful of words,
> even the miraculous ones.
> For the miraculous we do our best.
> Sometimes they swarm like insects
> and leave not a sting but a kiss.
> They can be as good as fingers.
> They can be as trusty as the rock
> you stick your bottom on.
> But they can be both daisies and bruises.
>
> Yet I am in love with words.
> They are doves falling out of the ceiling.
> They are six holy oranges sitting in my lap.
> They are the trees, the legs of summer,
> and the sun, its passionate face.
>
> Yet often they fail me.
> I have so much I want to say,

The Words

so many stories, images, proverbs, etc.
But the words aren't good enough,
the wrong ones kiss me.
Sometimes I fly like an eagle
but with the wings of a wren.

But I try to take care
and be gentle to them.
Words and eggs must be handled with care.
Once broken they are impossible
things to repair.
  "Words," *The Awful Rowing Toward God* (Boston:
  Houghton Mifflin Company, 1975), 71.

"Be careful of words, even the miraculous ones." It is
urgent advice for anyone whose mouth is open at the
liturgy. Do we recognize how words function here? Do
we, like this poet, have any awe for words? Do we treat
them as mere conveyors of information or feeling, or
only as sounds to go with the notes? Be careful of
words. Be hard on them. Don't settle for those that
cannot bear the weight.

Those who minister at the liturgy have to know why words matter, know why "Have a nice day" splinters under the weight of liturgy and "Go in peace to love and serve the Lord" just might hold.

The following texts from the writings of Abraham Joshua Heschel are a summons to attend to our words. Like much of his writing, it can itself be savored and returned to for clarity.

The Words

What, as a rule, makes it possible for us to pray is our ability to affiliate our own minds with the pattern of fixed texts, to unlock our hearts to the words, and to surrender to their meanings. The words stand before us as living entities full of spiritual power, of a power which often surpasses the grasp of our minds. The words are often the givers, and we the recipients. They inspire our minds and awaken our hearts. Most of us do not know the answer to one of the most important questions, namely, What is our ultimate concern? We do not know what to pray for. It is the liturgy that teaches us what to pray for. It is through the words of the liturgy that we discover what moves us unawares, what is urgent in our lives, what in us is related to the ultimate. . . . Carried away on the wings of praying words, we are at once in a sphere where our thoughts may be released from the pitiful prison of the platitudes of self and be led to a sphere in which we may exchange grief for hope, thought for light. . . . It is good that there are words sanctified by ages of worship, by the honesty and love of generations. If it were left to ourselves, who would know what word is right to be offered as praise in the sight of the God or which of our perishable thoughts is worthy of entering eternity? *Man's Quest for God* (New York: Charles Scribner's Sons, 1954), 31–32.

It is not enough, therefore, to articulate a sound. Unless one understands that the word is stronger than the will; unless one knows how to approach a word with all the joy, the hope or the grief we own, prayer will hardly come to pass. The words must not fall off our lips like dead leaves in the autumn. They must rise like birds out of the heart into the vast expanse of eternity. . . . In our own civilization, in which so much is being done for the cause of the liquidation of language, the realm of prayer is like an arsenal for the spirit, where words are kept clean, holy, full of power. . . . A word of prayer is like a strap we take hold of when tottering in a rushing streetcar which seems to be turning over.   *Man's Quest for God, 27.*

Novelist John Updike says it another way in *Rabbit Is Rich:*

Laugh at ministers all you want: they have the words we need to hear, the ones the dead have spoken.

What must we learn of our words, the words that sometimes "swarm" and "kiss," the words that we need to hear because they are "the ones the dead have spoken," the words that are the straps we hold in this teetering streetcar that is our world, the words that are "trusty as the rock you stick your bottom on"?

Liturgy's words must be like that, but what has happened to words in the liturgy? They abound, spoken and sung. To that, anyone can testify. Some of them are strong, chosen, cared for. Too often even the well-chosen, well-said words are not paced carefully and are not surrounded by any silence. The surrounding environment, our whole culture, makes it difficult to know words in the way that ritual demands, to love and treasure words, to know how precious and how powerful they are.

There are some practical things to be said to musicians about words. The most practical has been urged already: Learn to love good words, learn to care for them, to keep them (as Heschel says) "clean, holy, full of power." But that cannot happen just in the liturgy while we leave our day-by-day sense for words to be dictated by the culture. Nor will the liturgy be made of easy sentiment or the clichés of religious or secular life. Caring for words means listening and it means reading. Listen to the speech of those who use our marvelous language well. This is not listening for memorable phrases but listening for what language sounds like when it is treasured and reverenced. We'll rarely find this on radio or television. Many who speak with this authority probably do not reflect much on their words and language, but they—and they are often the poor and sometimes children—have a love and an awe of words that saves the language from becoming idle chatter on the one hand or mere transmission of information on the other.

One who serves the liturgy with song—cantor, music coordinator, choir member—must be a careful listener, trying to catch, through all the babble, the strength of right words well spoken. It is hard work to cultivate a right love of words, to be such an intense listener, to build slowly a delight in words themselves and all that they can be and do. The musician does it not simply to be able to discriminate, to choose the strong words over the weak in a hymn or other text, but so that the good words chosen can be loved, savored, treasured, repeated, taken into the whole soul and mind and heart as they are taken into the whole tongue and lips and throat. It is a discipline, though a very natural and human discipline, to care for words in this way.

Words must also be read because listening only gets us so far. What do people read today? One would try not to judge only from the tabloids and large-print magazines by the checkout counters or from the paperbacks that are on the drugstore racks. Can we find and spend time with the words that challenge, draw us out, open up realms, give names to reality? The musician who serves the assembly has this task: to spend time with the language at its best, to gradually get to be at home there, to become the disciple of those who have written the poetry and stories and essays. This has nothing to do with seeking out resources for the liturgy. It has to do with a ministry. The musician serves a sort of lifelong apprenticeship to those who can show us respect for words, the dignity of words, the wonder of language.

The assembly is well served when those who do any of the ministries that enable singing can themselves be seen, whether at the liturgy or away from it, to demand much of words and to show great gratitude and respect for such a gift.

Most of the texts we sing at liturgy are acclamations and psalms and litanies; their words are from approved translations or compositions. We may sometimes feel that a better translation could have been made, a better original text composed; little by little this is coming about. It is well to be critical of these texts where they are lacking, but also well to immerse ourselves in their words, to treat them—for all they might lack—as the words with which we sing as the church. They are the words which rehearse us so that we sound—not just at liturgy but always—like baptized people are meant to sound. "Lord, have mercy," "Lord, hear our prayer," "Holy, holy, holy Lord! Heaven and earth are full of your glory!" "Amen," "Alleluia," "Thanks be to God"—these and the other texts we know by heart are a sort of measure of all our other words. These are the language we speak, words that are "clean, holy, full of power." At home in such words, we begin to know how to look at any other texts that propose themselves for the assembly.

Among the words which we have kept central to the singing of the liturgy are the psalms. For Jews and Christians who pray and who take part in communal worship, the psalms are the way we learn the language of prayer. For musicians, they are the songs by which all other song must be measured.

One of the most significant elements of the revision of the Roman Rite of the Mass following Vatican Council II has been the restoration of psalmody. The psalm is a regular part of the eucharistic liturgy after the first reading, but it is also an option for entrance and communion processions. Yet in many places psalmody has not become part of the people's ritual. Sometimes the psalm is recited by a lector as if it were another scripture reading. Sometimes the psalm is omitted in favor of something else that can be sung (sometimes these are compositions "based on" a psalm, but most of them are based on psalms the way plastic ferns are based on living ones). The restoration of psalmody to the Sunday liturgy can mean a restoration of psalmody to the Christian people. The lectionary has offered the possibility of using the same psalm Sunday after Sunday (the "seasonal responsorial psalms") so that these can become a part of what we know by heart, can in fact begin to be our own words, the words that teach us how to talk and pray as Christians. Instead, most parishes take the option of having a different psalm every Sunday with a refrain that will not be heard again for three years—and no one gets any words or any melody into heart and soul.

The Words

Musicians ought to wrap themselves in our psalms, little by little exploring the pages of the psalter. Take the seasonal psalms for starters, find musical settings that really sing and use them day by day in morning and evening prayers. Treat these words like the words of a script to be committed to memory. Treat them like the words of the character you have been assigned to play in life, for that is what they are. (The same can be said, of course, of the canticles and the Lord's Prayer—all compositions of persons who knew their psalms!) Heschel's words again are so to the point: "We do not know what to pray for. It is the liturgy that teaches us what to pray for. It is through the words of the liturgy that we discover what moves us unawares, what is urgent in our lives, what in us is related to the ultimate. . . . It is good that there are words sanctified by ages of worship, by the honesty and love of generations." We and our generation do not have all the words, all the ideas. We stand in a great procession: We must learn the chant, make it our own, hand it on. This does nothing to belittle what our own compositions must be. In fact, it is a measure.

Were we faithful to the psalms as a standard for our own new words, we would approach with great caution and great zeal for excellence those times which the Sunday liturgy allows for hymns and songs: the entrance rite, the processions, the concluding rite. We are speaking here about words only, though certainly judgments must also be made about the quality and the appropriateness of the music (that is: Is it good as music? And if so, is it the right kind of music for a communion procession?).

What dangers are there with the words? With the psalms as our teachers, we can name the great modern errors as kitsch and cliché.

The Unbearable Lightness of Being, a novel by Milan Kundera, is about the reign of kitsch in the modern world: the triumph of kitsch over communism and capitalism alike. In one scene, a woman who has left her native Czechoslovakia visits the United States and is taken for a drive by a senator. They stop to watch a lovely scene of children playing in a field:

Sitting behind the wheel and gazing dreamily after the
four little bounding figures, he said to Sabina, "Just
look at them. . . . Now that's what I call happiness."

The storyteller reflects:

The senator had only one argument in his favor: his
feeling. When the heart speaks, the mind finds it
indecent to object. In the realm of kitsch, the
dictatorship of the heart reigns supreme. . . . Kitsch
causes two tears to flow in quick succession. The first
tear says: How nice to see children running on the
grass! The second tear says: How nice to be moved,
together with all mankind, by children running on the
grass! It is the second tear that makes kitsch. *The
Unbearable Lightness of Being* (New York: Harper and
Row, 1984), 250.

We must watch out for that second tear. We must watch
out for the dictatorship of the heart—not just in the
Hallmark store, but in the missalette. It has nothing to do
with the human condition except its denial. We are

people who worship at a table where we declare
ourselves bound to a communion that is as far from
"Let there be peace on earth and let it begin with me"
as it is from "God bless America." It is! Or else the
broken bread and the poured out cup are telling lies,
and then indeed we do need to paraphrase the psalms.
"Kitsch," Kundera writes, "is a folding screen set up to
curtain off death." A weekly hour of kitsch may be
popular, may keep folks smiling and coming back. It
works for the TV evangelists and it can work for us.
But it has nothing to do with a church bound to Jesus
and Israel. Aidan Kavanagh has written that any such
liturgy "seems to reflect a kind of euphoric optimism
unwarranted by a steady hold on reality" (*Elements of
Rite*, 99). How true this is of the words that fill the
songbooks of the last two decades.

The Words

But the psalms never screen off death and their only
optimism comes from an almost incredible grip on
reality: They just can't get enough of it. These psalms
have schooled the great hymn writers of the Christian
tradition, from the ancient compositions ("O radiant

light, O sun divine") through the medieval texts
("Creator of the stars of night") and the texts of the
Reformation ("A mighty fortress is our God") to the
best of contemporary writing for the liturgy. The ways
of expression change, but not the demand for honesty
with our words. Of those who would compose texts
today we must ask what has been asked of the
psalmists, what Kavanagh called that "steady hold on
reality." That indeed may come from artists who have
looked at this culture more clearly than the rest of
us—and have news to tell us.

Those who choose music for liturgy should come
to the task disciplined by their engagement with
the words of psalms and other texts of the tradition.
The test for any text to be sung at liturgy must be both
the strength of its poetry and the fidelity (to our
scriptures, to our liturgy) of its meaning. No kitsch.

All the words must be good enough to be there time
after time. For some words this means each Sunday,

for others all the Sundays of a season, for others the appropriate Sundays of Ordinary Time, for others just once a year (but each year!). The need is not endless. For the liturgy to belong to the assembly, the repertory must be limited. It can grow, evolve, but only when the priority is an assembly singing their liturgy. There is hardly room then for words that cannot carry through, cannot be there time after time to interpret our world and lives. It is difficult but important to demand of our words at liturgy what the culture has practically ceased to ask of all its speakers (advertisers, politicians, teachers, "stars"): passion, simplicity, the capacity to be there again and again to put names on all of reality.

Those who choose music must accustom themselves to demanding such qualities of the text. Poor texts abound, but there are enough good, strong texts to begin building the repertory of any assembly. We simply do not need the poor texts. Contemporary compositions should have to meet far higher standards than their publishers are likely to apply. The needs of the assembly are limited needs and the possible repertory is a limited repertory. Every place we give to inferior and unworthy words is a place not given to strong words.

Consider, for example, these simple and direct words by an early 19th century American poet:

> What wondrous love is this, O my soul, O my soul?
> What wondrous love is this, O my soul?
> What wondrous love is this that caused
>   the Lord of bliss
>
> To bear the dreadful curse for my soul, for my soul;
> To bear the dreadful curse for my soul?
>
> To God and to the Lamb I will sing, I will sing;
> To God and to the Lamb, I will sing;
> To God and to the Lamb who is the great I Am,
> While millions join the theme, I will sing, I will sing;
> While millions join the theme, I will sing.
>
> And when from death I'm free, I'll sing on, I'll sing on;
> And when from death I'm free, I'll sing on;
> And when from death I'm free, I'll sing and joyful be,

And through eternity I'll sing on, I'll sing on!
And through eternity, I'll sing on.

Some might say, "Where's the message?" That's a very good question when we look at texts but not as easy as it appears. Like rite itself, and like *all* the words of our rites, the words of our songs are not intended to be snappy slogans advertising this spirituality or that gospel-based politics. The good words are those that shape us in light of the gospel and its liturgy, shape and form us in this way: that over the many, many times we sing them they do not wear out but become our own dear and cherished vocabulary. They do all those things that Heschel and Sexton and Updike told us about words. Message? We are the message.

There might also be the objection to these words: "Look at all that first-person singular? What kind of a church would be so self-centered?" That also is a good but often oversimplified question. The easier answer is: Go and read Psalm 51 or 130 or the Magnificat or so many other foundational texts. It is not that the pronoun "I" should not be heard. That pronoun is not what makes a piece deny that for us we stand before God, are called by God, as church. There are modern songs aplenty with "we" subjects and "us" objects that know nothing of the church. The question is not "I" or "we," but what happens to this text in the mouths of the assembly. What happens when each year it is their concluding song on the Sundays of November?

Those responsible need to look carefully at specific moments within the ritual. If we hold that our song is not just background music to "the real liturgy," but *is* the liturgy, then appropriateness is crucial. For example, what is needed for communion (and how does it differ from what is needed for other moments in the liturgy)? What are the good texts old and new?

In considering words for the communion procession, we can take our starting point from the ritual itself and from how this has been done in the church's tradition. It is a time to sing without books or leaflet, a time when the body must be free to move and the hands free to take bread and cup. The church once did what was natural here in giving the assembly a refrain to sing while the cantor or choir sang the verses of a psalm. That remains valid today. It also points us toward other music that can be handled by an assembly as their own without any need to look at text. Again, however, we are faced with an abundance of contemporary texts that offer refrains or choruses for the assembly, but whose words do not measure up. Some few texts have that wonderful ambiguity that draws the singers in the first time and the thousandth time:

> Eat this bread, drink this cup,
> come to me and never be hungry.
> Eat this bread, drink this cup,
> trust in me and you will not thirst.

Like many of the other compositions that have come from the community of Taizé in France, this asks us to dwell again and again in the words of the scripture, to make our home there. An assembly would not need dozens of communion songs, but only one or two for each of the seasons and several good ones for Ordinary Time. Beyond that, the choir or cantor or organist may be at home, but the people will not be.

This particular example does speak of the ritual it accompanies. That is by no means necessary with a communion song. The use of various psalms and their refrains at communion shows that word and ritual activity need not define one another literally. They may work through a sort of juxtaposition, as when the communion song is Psalm 23 sung by a cantor with the assembly singing the refrain, "My shepherd is the Lord. Nothing indeed shall I fear." Likewise, the African text "Jesu, Jesu, fill us with your love" or Taizé's "Jesus, remember me" can be appropriate communion songs though they never describe the gesture of holy communion.

In all of these examples, it is hardly possible to separate words and melody. That is as it should be, of course. The best words will go nowhere if the tune does not invite singing and repeating. For our purposes here, we have focused on words. The musician's focus must always go beyond.

Words must be examined also with an eye for the images they present of God and of ourselves. Much work is being done so that we might sing words that speak inclusively of humankind. This involves sensitivity to terms that exclude women, but it also involves a far wider sensitivity to a bias in our texts that is more subtle than the "he's" and "mankind's." Working with old texts and writing new ones is challenging work and is not for everyone. Much of what has been done to remedy the situation is unsatisfactory as poetry. A showy inclusivity in texts that lack the strength and beauty demanded for communal use in liturgy does no one any good.

We are challenged to avoid lyrics about God that speak only with masculine pronouns and that never stray beyond very narrow and usually stereotypical masculine qualities. A prolonged, steady dedication can produce a parish repertory that is rich in images of God and includes new texts as well as old.

These word problems often begin to sensitize the musician to yet other difficulties. For example, the words to "Lord of the Dance" bring back some of Christianity's worst instincts in portraying the Jewish people.

All of this about words must be bound within the caution and the reminder: Nearly all the words we sing at liturgy are given for us by the liturgy. We do not have to search for the right words to answer in song to "The Lord be with you." We do not have to search to find how to acclaim with earth and heaven as the eucharistic prayer begins, continues, ends. The litanies of penitential rite, of intercession, of the breaking of the bread, all are largely written, at least the assembly's part. The psalms and refrains, including the seasonal options, are there in the lectionary. Good music we must find, but the words

are there and these words are the foundation of the
assembly's singing. In their current translations into
English, not all of these are as fine as they might be,
but that will come. They are the words that must be
sung. They are *the* vocabulary of prayer for this
church. Without these words, in familiar and strong
tunes, we cannot have the church doing its liturgy.
Without them, the other singing can be no more than a
pious sing-along at best. The musician, then, before all
the quests after new or old words for hymns, is
devoted to finding and offering to the assembly these
words of acclamation, litany and psalm.

Silence
and Pace

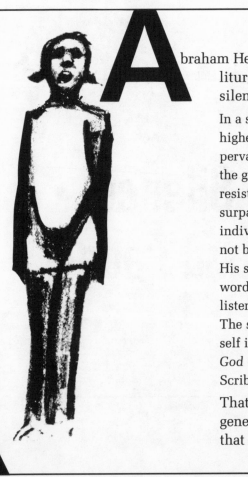

Abraham Heschel wrote that in liturgy even speech is silence.

In a sense, our liturgy is a higher form of silence. It is pervaded by an awed sense of the grandeur of God which resists description and surpasses all expression. The individual is silent. He does not bring forth his own words. His saying the consecrated words is in essence an act of listening to what they convey. The spirit of Israel speaks, the self is silent. *Man's Quest for God* (New York: Charles Scribner's Sons, 1954), 44.

That is hard to take for a generation raised to believe that in liturgy the "self" is all that should speak, that anything else is artificial, bogus. Heschel is not restating an argument to treat the liturgy as magic ("Just say the right words in the right order and everything will take care of itself"), but he is arguing that at liturgy we are listeners. In one important sense, liturgy always finds us silent, listening even to the words we ourselves speak.

The enemy of this sort of silence is not speech at all, but haste. Brian Helge, in speaking of the time it must take for the long series of scripture readings at the Easter Vigil, puts it simply: "Haste will stop your ears." And that is the truth. That is why in our liturgy we cannot be hasty. We need not be long, but we cannot be hasty.

Silence itself is called for a number of times within the eucharistic rite and at corresponding times in our other rites. All who minister to the assembly at liturgy need to be clear about this silence: It is a stillness. It is not a chance to get ready for the next piece of music, nor a time even to think ahead. It is stillness of hand and eyes as well as lips. These silent times come after the invitation to prayer ("Let us pray"), after each of the first two readings, after the homily, after communion. But these rubrics which call for silence are only an indication of what must be in the bones of the assembly, including the ministers: a sense for the pace, a sense for how we do this thing together, how moment relates to moment.

That is what we so often lack. Without it, so much good effort is lost. This sense for the pace of doing liturgy is learned by repeated participation in the liturgy well celebrated, but that means—for those who prepare the liturgy—care and vigilance that all ministers acquire and act out of a disciplined effort to get the flow of the rite into their muscles and minds. It has to become for them something more than "knowing when my part comes," or remembering that the sign of the cross comes before the greeting without any sense for how the two relate. A sense for the pace of liturgy means identifying that relation of sign of the

**Silence
and Pace**

cross and greeting, not historically or theologically,
but rather ritually. How is part of our deed at ritual to
let the one follow the other? Good efforts with music,
preaching and in most every other art that contributes
to liturgy are turned into entertainment or edification
when the ministers and assembly have no habit of
good pacing, no hard-learned and well-disciplined
feel for the flow of the liturgy. It is that flow that
demands and creates silence.

Do we yet have a sense for what an entrance rite—
that is, the entrance of the whole assembly into its
liturgy, not of the ministers into the assembly—is to
be for us? Do we know in an almost physical way what
is the movement of the liturgy of the word or the
liturgy of the eucharist? "Know" here means not just
familiarity as one is familiar with the flow of a
commercial seen a hundred times, but "know" is like
the knowledge one has of dressing oneself or eating
and drinking in company. Without the knowledge in
the bones, a habitual freedom for care and beauty in
the deed are impossible. An entrance rite or a

communion rite has an order and that order brings with it a pace. When we are at home with this, then haste is not even a question. And there is room for silence.

Coming down to cases, then, how long is a silence? That too is an art as is told in the story of the pianist who was praised for how well the notes were handled. The pianist replied: "Anyone can handle the notes, but the spaces between the notes! That is the art." One practical thing to be said in parish liturgy is this: If the liturgy is to belong to the assembly, the length of the silent times cannot be the whim of the presider or musician and so be subject to change at every Mass. Rather, there needs to be a parish norm. Then the assembly is secure in the silence, takes possession of it (or it of them).

"The self is silent," Heschel said. The times of complete silence and stillness in the assembly are few. Heschel's point is that we are silent at liturgy in a larger sense: We put on our lips the words of the community, of the tradition, and so even in speaking we are silent listeners. Our own self is silent, filling with the words that are rehearsal of our role, our part in the life of the world. So in our rites we have the times of actual silence and these may be, surprisingly, the times when we do speak! That silent speech of ours comes from the profound listening that is to pervade the singing and speaking and moving of all the other moments of our rite.

Chapter 7

The Music
We Need

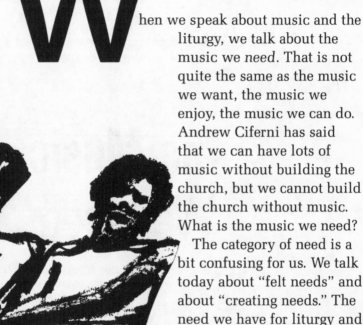

When we speak about music and the liturgy, we talk about the music we *need*. That is not quite the same as the music we want, the music we enjoy, the music we can do. Andrew Ciferni has said that we can have lots of music without building the church, but we cannot build the church without music. What is the music we need?

The category of need is a bit confusing for us. We talk today about "felt needs" and about "creating needs." The need we have for liturgy and its music does not come from such images, but from the way we need sleep, food, friends. That is to the point: not that we want it, like it, are obliged to it, but that we need it.

Whether we speak of eucharist on Sunday, or of morning or evening prayer, or of the burial or the wedding, a people doing their rites *need* music. We are not dealing with what would be pretty, what would be comfortable, what would enhance, what would create a proper mood. Maybe we are talking about *what would make it bearable.* Our rites do not really exist apart from such music. In truth, do anyone's? Does any tribe do its rituals without music? Music is practically invented in the need for rhythmic action, in the need to let the voice get beyond its tiny speaking range, in the need to let the words and moans and cheers too be all sorts of paces. Consider then the music we need.

We need the music that can be called acclamation. It has roots in the ritual shout and its simplest expression is "Amen." It is a sort of punctuation that gives shape and meaning to the text that is being proclaimed by the one presiding.

The eucharistic prayer is one place we experience acclamation. This is not a long monologue with pauses for song, but it is proclaimed text and acclamation together, neither able to stand apart from the other. To the ear they are woven together, one fabric then, a whole. If either is missing, there is no fabric, only random threads. Acclamation also comes in the alleluias of the gospel procession, in the "Thanks be to God" of the concluding rites, in the words sung to each person emerging from the baptismal pool, in the affirmation when a couple's marriage vows have been heard.

Some have tried to use applause as a contemporary acclamation, and at times it may be that. But some caution is needed because applause is too easily felt as an audience's response to something well done, and at liturgy we have no audience. Applause can too easily be a response to an event, whereas acclamation is essential to the event.

Parish musicians need to find that fairly small number of acclamations which all can know by heart. Variety here should be the variety that fits the seasons and feasts and not the variety between the early morning liturgy and the "main" liturgy. Then all ministers involved need to work and practice together so that at every liturgy ("That's just the way we do it here," people should say to their amazed and delighted guests) the acclamations belong to the assembly and come forth with integrity to create the liturgy. What would be the regular experience of such liturgy? Would the people to whom such liturgy belonged become people who would know how to acclaim God and God's goodness and justice day by day?

Our failure with acclamations in the eucharistic prayer can perhaps be seen in how quickly people seem to accept the "priestless Sunday" where a deacon or a lay person leads the liturgy of the word and communion service. Would not people whose experience was of the eucharistic prayer as climax of their Sunday assembly be more anxious to hold onto it? We went very quickly from knowing the eucharistic prayer as a sort of shrine for the all-important words of consecration to knowing it hardly at all, just a long part for the priest with a little singing. The fault is partly in the text, but even with present texts much more can be done to integrate acclamations. Simply teaching about the eucharistic prayer will not lead to vital practice. We have to do it, presiders and musicians exercising their muscles till they are disciplined in the proper pace and rhythm.

Another music we need is the litany, the pattern of call and response with the former ever changing and the latter ever staying the same. At the eucharist and at our other rites this comes in various expressions: the penitential rite, the prayers of intercession, the Lamb of God, the traditional litanies (of the saints, the Holy Name, Loreto). The litany is, like the acclamation, a "by heart" music. It needs to be sung for its words must be patterned, must come over and over again in rhythms, mantra-like, so that the whole gradually gathers us up in a deed that is more than the sum of the individual "calls."

There must be a certain length to litanies. This will vary, but in each case there should be enough time to enter into the rhythm of refrain, the back and forth with the leader. Though each text of the leader in a litany should be chosen or written carefully, it is not really the leader's texts that make a litany do its work. Rather, it is the repetition of response and call, the play of the rhythm itself in which participants become the church interceding.

We need psalms. Assemblies need refrains that have become very much their own through seasons of use. The psalms are even more the makings of morning and evening prayer, the prayer of all Christians. The lively presence of the psalm at eucharist will depend on there being other psalms, just a few, as familiar prayers for beginning and ending the day—for everyone.

100

Acclamations, litanies, psalms. These are what we most need to do our liturgy. The needs beyond these three are modest. Hymns have a small but important place in the liturgies of the Roman tradition; they are most at home in the liturgy of the hours. We are heirs to a great richness of hymnody, a large part of it from outside the Roman tradition. With new and old hymns we nearly hid the musical needs of the eucharist during the last decades. Now we seek the constrained but important place hymns should have. When a hymn is chosen, it should not be too quickly dismembered, leaving many verses unsung. In some cases it is possible to omit part of the text. However, when the hymn has been constructed as a whole, it should be respected and sung from beginning to end.

The Music We Need

In speaking of the music we need, the difficult thing is this: The liturgy is not something we invent week by week. It is not ours in that sense at all. We receive and make our own and then hand on. Yet for liturgy to be liturgy at all, it must be entirely ours. We live in that paradox.